D1549898

DROITWICH

700039934466

500
ACRYLIC
MIXES

DORDOGNE FOREST
(PREVIOUS PAGE)

Yellow-greens are fragmented by the purple-blue shadows, to make the most of the complementary contrast (see page 48).

PATIO
(LEFT)

Red and green complementary colours are used to good effect in this painting of a dappled patio.

500
ACRYLIC
MIXES

SHARON FINMARK

BATSFORD

First published in the United Kingdom in 2012 by
Batsford
10 Southcombe Street
London W14 0RA

An imprint of Anova Books Company Ltd

Copyright © Batsford, 2012
Text and illustrations © Sharon Finmark, 2012

The moral rights of the author have been asserted.

All rights reserved. No part of this publication may be reproduced or stored in a retrieval system for commercial purposes, without the prior written permission of the copyright owner.

ISBN 9781849940467

A CIP catalogue record for this book is available from the British Library.

20 19 18 17 16 15 14 13 12
10 9 8 7 6 5 4 3 2 1

Reproduction by Mission Productions Ltd, Hong Kong
Printed by 1010 Printing International, China

This book can be ordered direct from the publisher at the website www.anovabooks.com, or try your local bookshop.

LOW HILL LANDSCAPE

Paint is applied in layers of thinned acrylics to make one area blend into another. The fields in the distance have more intensely built-up coloured layers.

Contents

INTRODUCTION

Acrylic paints are popular with many artists for their versatility. Their advantage over oil paints is the rapid and uniform speed of drying, and because they are water-based they don't require the use of mediums such as oil and turpentine. Yet unlike watercolours, they allow the artist to put down layers of colour in rapid succession, making exciting paintings with vibrancy and distinct brushmarks.

Understanding colour

While we all have a personal response to colour, it's generally accepted that certain colours have a particular psychological impact on everyone. This means that artists, while using a palette that suits their own preferences, can deploy colour to draw an emotional response from the viewer.

Acrylics are associated with opacity and intense flat colour, and it is not always realized that they can be diluted with water to produce delicate washes. These are not as mobile as watercolour and dry more quickly, but once you become accustomed to handling them you will find them very useful for changing a colour underneath and also for transparency as a contrast to the solidity of the heavier acrylic marks.

The colours in the tubes invite you to use them just as they are, but you will soon want to mix your own colours too. Indeed, you should resist the temptation to buy a wide range of pigments, however exciting they may look; a painting benefits from the coherence that comes from using a limited range of colours, so it's better to choose carefully and mix the extra colours you need.

COLOUR-MIX SAMPLES (ABOVE)

Try your mixes on a rough piece of paper to ensure you have the right colour before applying to your painting.

WALKING FIGURE (RIGHT)

Loose brushstrokes and broken marks of green and red give the impression of movement, which a solid colour would fail to suggest.

THE LANGUAGE OF COLOUR

The terms employed to describe paint can be confusing at first, but don't let that worry you – just seeing what the colours do as you use them will help to make everything clear. The terms below are ones you will commonly encounter.

Achromatic Lacking true colour; black, white and grey are considered to be achromatic, or neutral.

Adjacent/analogous The colours that neighbour each other on the colour wheel; for example, a colour scheme that used reds, oranges and yellows would be described as analogous.

Colour family Colours of the same hue, such as the range of reds or of blues.

Complementary The colours that are opposite each other on the colour wheel, such as yellow and violet (see page 48).

High key/low key Bright, light colours are described as high key, while subdued, dark ones are low key (see pages 152–155).

Hue The name of the colour, such as yellow or blue.

Monochromatic A painting made with just one colour in different tonal values, such as a range of blues.

Neutral Greys, browns, earth colours and similar mixes are known as neutrals (see page 140).

Saturation The intensity of a colour.

Shade A darker colour of the original hue.

Tint A colour lightened with white.

Tone The lightness or darkness of a colour. All colours have tone, and some will always be lighter than others; the deepest yellow will not be as dark as a deep blue, for example, but a paler blue can be the same tone as a yellow. Making black and white photocopies of colours is a good way to understand this.

Value How light or dark in tone a colour appears.

Ways of mixing acrylics

Most acrylic sets contain two pigments in each of the primary colours (red, yellow and blue), one warm and one cool. The concept of warm and cool colours is important, as it is fundamental to successful colour mixing. Cadmium Red, Cadmium Yellow and Ultramarine are warm, while Alizarin Crimson, Prussian Blue and Lemon Yellow are cool (see page 34). These are the colours you should get to know best and the ones you should use for your first exciting experiments in colour mixing.

There are two ways for artists to mix acrylic paints, each of which produces a different effect.

PALETTE MIXING

By mixing pigments in the palette you can achieve the colour you require before applying the mix to paper. By altering the proportions of the pigments in the mix, the range of colours you can achieve is almost limitless.

Cadmium Red + Cadmium Yellow =

Lemon Yellow + Prussian Blue =

Ultramarine + Alizarin Crimson =

Cadmium Red + Cadmium Yellow   Lemon Yellow + Prussian Blue   Ultramarine + Alizarin Crimson

OVERLAYING

In this method of mixing, a glaze of one colour is laid over a dry area of another to produce a third colour. Additional layers can intensify or alter the mix as required.

1 BEFORE YOU START

For a novice painter an art-supplies shop is an exciting and slightly bewildering place, stocked with all sorts of tempting paints, surfaces and accessories. However, the best advice is always to start small, with the best-quality materials you can afford, and to become familiar with them and with the techniques described in this chapter before splashing out on extra pigments, brushes and other equipment.

Materials

Acrylic paints come in three different types: soft body, heavy body and super-heavy body, ranging from a runny consistency to a thick, buttery one that will give texture and show brushmarks. Which you use is a matter of choice and what you feel suits a particular subject, but as you can thicken soft-body pigments with impasto gel and dilute heavy-bodied ones with water you will never be left high and dry without the consistency you want.

To apply the paint you can use either synthetic or natural-hair brushes; choose firm bristles for thick paint and softer brushes for thinner consistencies.

DORDOGNE FOREST

The colour was mixed on the surface of the unstretched canvas. The streaks of Lemon Yellow and green on the ground were still damp when the shadows were put in, thus blending well. The foreground is very warm orange applied across the damp yellow.

Grounds

As long as you avoid oil-based and shiny surfaces you can apply acrylics to almost any support. You will need to prepare all surfaces, except mountboard and watercolour and acrylic papers, with acrylic gesso primer, to which you can add pigment to give you a coloured ground that will complement your painting.

MOROCCAN LANDSCAPE
(LEFT)

Reds and blues dominate this painting, in which I was playing with warm and cool colours. However, the main focus was to let the white ground come through between the brushstrokes, giving a feeling of sharp contrasts to the painting.

HAMPSTEAD HEATH
(BELOW)

To lay a pinkish ground that would convey a warm autumnal day, I used a touch of red in the white primer. The red also appears in the foliage, the repeated the colour making the whole composition coherent.

STORMY SKY
(ABOVE)

Here, the top of the painting was blue and the lower half Burnt Sienna. Once these were dry, I painted on top of them, letting them show through here and there. Although not technically a ground, they formed a base on which to work.

Palettes

You will find a large array of palettes on sale in art-supply shops, and you probably have old saucers and similar receptacles at home that could be used for mixing paint on – even cheap, disposable plastic dishes will suffice, as long as they are white.

However, the usefully fast speed with which acrylics dry on the painting surface is less conveniently mirrored by how rapidly the mixes dry on the palette. This means that once you have got a mix just right you are liable to find that before long you have to start remixing carefully to reproduce an exact match with the paint you have already applied. So, unless you habitually paint very quickly, you need to buy or make a stay-wet palette.

Several manufacturers of art materials offer these, and while they vary in the exact design, they have all been developed to keep the paint workable and moist. They consist of a lidded plastic tray lined with a sheet of absorbent paper, or sometimes a sponge, that can be soaked in water. On top of this is a sheet of membrane paper which acts as the palette surface and draws up moisture from the absorbent material below. As long as you keep the lid of the container shut, your paint will remain usable for several days.

Once you have finished with the membrane, discard it and lay on a fresh piece, topping up the absorbent paper beneath with water as you do so.

WOMAN DRAWING

A great deal of Burnt Sienna was used, both as a primer and in the mixes, so a stay-wet palette was essential to store the mixes while the painting was completed.

MAKING A STAY-WET PALETTE

You will find it very easy to make your own stay-wet palette rather than buying a ready-made one, and it is a much more economical way to proceed. Buying rolls of kitchen paper and greaseproof paper from a supermarket will mean you have a generous supply of replacement membrane that doesn't require making a visit to a specialist shop to replenish.

1 You will need a shallow plastic container with an airtight lid such as is used to store food.

2 Dampen a sheet of kitchen paper under the tap.

3 Line the bottom of the container with the dampened kitchen paper.

4 Cut a sheet of kitchen paper, greaseproof paper or tracing paper to fit the container.

5 Lay the paper on top of the dampened kitchen paper to act as your palette.

Acrylic techniques

Because acrylic paints dry so rapidly, they suit a working method of applying layers of colour in rapid succession without disturbing the underlayers. Blending is possible while the paint is still wet, but it must be done very swiftly; if you want to show a graduated shadow you will need to blend the range of tone as you go, in order to achieve subtlety. On the other hand, if you like big, bold shapes of colour, acrylic paints offer you a perfect edge after only a brief wait for one colour to dry before putting another against it.

Whatever the subject may be, the approach is always to start with dark colours and work the lights in towards the end. For example, if the subject is a landscape with light flickering on the trees, the main body of the trees is painted first, with lighter colours placed on top.

For the natural world, including skies, broken brushmarks are excellent for conveying soft, variable surfaces. Flat areas of colour with overlays or glazes are effective for buildings before you start to put in architectural details, while impasto (see page 21) and scratching out (see page 25) create areas of interesting texture to hold the viewer's attention.

ADDING TEXTURE

A rough surface will break up the paint marks, creating interesting results. Try applying textured gel or sand to wet gesso primer so that it adheres as the primer dries. For coarser textures, such as fine wood shavings, lay a first coat of primer and then a coat of PVA glue before adding the texture. Add a final layer of primer once the glue has dried.

NORFOLK SKY

The texture in this painting is created by adding granules from a texture paste for acrylics. They stick into the primed surface, then you just paint on top. The surface looks gritty but takes the paint effectively.

HIGHGATE FROM THE HEATH
(LEFT)

The watered-down foreground and sky of this painting gives a sense of place and atmosphere.

PATH ON THE HEATH
(RIGHT)

The trees in the distance were watered down to give perspective and the impression of distance.

WATERING DOWN

Thinning acrylic paint with water allows you to produce veils of colour for a delicate effect or to alter a colour by enhancing it slightly with a thin glaze of another colour laid on top. If you wish you can even glaze over the entire expanse of a painting, for example to mellow an evening landscape.

Experiment with different dilutions – the more water you add, the lighter the colour. The paint will not be as fluid as watercolour, but looks similar.

NUDE

The light and dark areas, strongly defined using thickly applied paint, show how impasto techniques are particularly suited to defining the shape and form of the body.

IMPASTO TECHNIQUE

This is a way of painting in which the pigment stands proud of the surface. It is more than adding texture using something like a texture medium; it is the paint itself that creates the texture.

Use a very dry flat bristle or synthetic brush loaded with paint to make strong, thickly applied marks. The expressive quality lends itself to almost any subject, the ridges and valleys of paint adding a sense of depth to the painting.

AMARYLLIS

The petals and the background were painted with thick, creamy acrylic and the rest of the painting was worked with thinner paint, creating a strong contrast to make the flowerheads stand out.

ADDING MATERIALS

Because acrylics are quick-drying they can often hold other materials. Anything bigger and more solid than a grain of rice may need to be stuck on first with PVA glue, but after that the paint covers it over and you can work on turning your two-dimensional surface into a three-dimensional one. But don't get too carried away – stick to small objects such as buttons, netting, lace and tissue paper.

RED AND PURPLE ABSTRACT

I added torn paper and crumpled tissue to the support before over painting with harmonious colours.

VARNISHING

Acrylics dry to a matt surface, but if you wish to have a gloss finish that resembles oils you can varnish your painting. Always use a varnish intended for acrylics, which will dry quickly to a clear film. This is available in both matt and gloss, and if you prefer a semi-matt finish you can simply mix the two together.

Lay the painting flat and apply the varnish in smooth strokes in one direction. Leave to dry overnight, then apply a second coat at right angles.

GRID ABSTRACT

Varnishing added another dimension to this broad brushstroke painting, giving depth to the colour and picking out the grooves of the marks on the surface.

SCUMBLING

This technique is a way of enlivening colour and is particularly effective with acrylics as it is done on a surface of dried paint – the rapidity of drying means there's no risk of picking up the undercolour as you work.

Load the brush with paint and lightly scrub it on to the first colour, using rough, loose strokes so that the undercolour is only partially obscured, giving an effect of shimmering modified colour. Using different colour temperatures will give a dramatic effect, while combining colours that are similar in temperature is more subtle.

JUGS

Rough watercolour paper works particularly well with scumbling techniques. The paint is distributed over the surface unevenly so that the undercolour shows through effectively.

SCRATCHING OUT

In effect, scratching out is drawing into the paint and as such is an excellent way of adding outlines, for example for field patterns or winter trees.

First lay an undercolour and leave it to dry, then paint another colour on top. Swiftly, before it dries, scratch into the surface to reveal the first colour, using any sharp point such as the handle of a brush, a painting knife, or an old credit card. As with scumbling, you can choose dramatic or subtle effects by your use of colour temperature.

NIGHT SKY
(ABOVE)

Scratching out lifts the intense colours and helps to define the patterns of the dark hillside.

WILD SKY
(LEFT)

Scratching out reveals the creamy yellow underpainting and introduces movement and rhythm into the stormy clouds.

2 YOUR BASIC PALETTE

The key to learning how to handle colour well is to begin by exploring a basic range of colours to see what you can make from various mixes and dilutions – there's no better way to gain the confidence that will allow you to paint fluently right from the very early stages of learning. Once using those pigments becomes second nature you can then give yourself a new challenge by extending the range with some extra colours to see what they will contribute to your paintings.

Arranging your palette

Always arrange the colours in your palette in the same order so that you can find the one you want quickly. There are three recommended ways to do this: following the order of the spectrum, with red, orange, yellow, green and blue running across the palette and black, white and the earth colours slightly separate; setting out the colours from light to dark; or putting warm colours on one side and cool on the other.

KITCHEN CORNER

Arranging the palette with warm colours on one side and cool on the other was a useful way to work with the strong contrasts in this painting.

Basic colours

A basic set of acrylic paints will usually contain Lemon Yellow, Cadmium Yellow, Cadmium Orange, Cadmium Red, Alizarin Crimson, Violet, Ultramarine, Prussian Blue, Hooker's Green, Viridian, Burnt Sienna, Yellow Ochre and Vandyke Brown, along with Black and White to offer you a range of different tints and shades.

As you have so many ways to mix the paints, these colours should provide an ample choice to create a huge variety of mixes, though you may wish to add a few more colours such as Permanent Rose, Cerulean, Cobalt Blue, Raw Umber and Burnt Umber.

Before you set about mixing pigments from your set to produce another colour, the first step is to assess the value of the colours. Some are initially dark in value, such as the blues, while others are light, such as the yellows. If you wish to lighten colours further, adding white paint will produce the desired result. While black will darken other colours, generally speaking a more lively effect will come from using the mixes shown in this book.

| Lemon Yellow | Cadmium Yellow | Cadmium Orange | Cadmium Red | Alizarin Crimson |

| Violet | Ultramarine | Prussian Blue | Hooker's Green | Viridian |

| Burnt Sienna | Yellow Ochre | Vandyke Brown | Black | White |

Black and White, with a touch of Ultramarine

Prussian Blue and White

Ultramarine

Yellow Ochre and Burnt Sienna

Cadmium Red and Cadmium Yellow

Hooker's Green

Lemon Yellow with a touch of Prussian Blue

Yellow Ochre scumbled over a Cadmium Yellow and Yellow Ochre mix

Cadmium Yellow and White

Lemon Yellow and Yellow Ochre mixed with Ultramarine

Alizarin Crimson and Ultramarine

CUBIST KITCHEN CORNER

PALETTE USED
Lemon Yellow
Cadmium Yellow
Cadmium Red
Alizarin Crimson
Ultramarine
Prussian Blue
Hooker's Green
Burnt Sienna
Yellow Ochre
Black
White

Lemon Yellow and White

White, with a touch of Yellow Ochre and Black mix

Dilutions

By diluting your pigments with water you will obtain a more transparent version of the original colour. Laying a very diluted colour over one that's already dry allows you to create a slightly different mix – for example, diluted blue laid over red will take on a purplish tinge.

Another effective way to use diluted colour is to add water gradually to create a subtle range of tones. For example, if you were painting a pillar lit from the side, the darker side would be the colour straight from the tube and then you would gently pull increasingly diluted colour across through the range of tones. This has to be done swiftly or the paint will dry to form a hard line.

If you find this too tricky at first, lay down the lightest, the most diluted paint first and then work your way towards the darkest tones to achieve the modulation you need. With practice you will be able to achieve a smooth graduation of tone.

Lemon Yellow

Cadmium Yellow

Cadmium Orange

Cadmium Red

Alizarin Crimson

Violet

Ultramarine

Prussian Blue

Hooker's Green

Viridian

Burnt Sienna

Yellow Ochre

Vandyke Brown

Black

Black and white

A painting that uses black and white only can be helpful as a tonal underpinning for a full-colour painting. A range of greys made by mixing Black and White will define the solidity of the subject and enable you to see the whole painting more clearly. Some artists use this as a plan for the final painting, while others paint over the top with colour.

Of course, you can also mix Black and White with colours as well as using them in monochrome. Adding White will obviously make the original colour lighter, whereas adding Black will make it darker and even change the colour (see page 146). Black has a deadening effect on strong colours,

reducing their intensity, and though that may sound an undesirable quality, in fact it can be very useful, if handled with caution. As for White, take care how much you use to create a lighter colour, as too much means your painting can look chalky.

To understand the impact of Black and White on other colours, make two colour charts, one with the addition of White and the other with the addition of Black, as shown on page 146. Take your time over it, watching the way the colours gradually change; you will find this really helpful as it takes a while to learn the quantities needed in order to produce what's in your mind's eye.

SHELVES

This painting was fun to do as the use of just Black and White made the way the light was influencing the tones very obvious. Playing around with the range of greys was the main focus of the painting. The china was mainly white, which helped to simplify the tones.

Primary colours

The term 'primary colours' is used for reds, blues and yellows because they cannot be mixed from other colours. In most small sets of paints there are usually two of each primary, plus some of the earth colours, such as the umbers and siennas.

The primary pigments will be supplied in a choice of warm and cool colours. While red is considered to be a hot colour and blue is cool, for example, they will have a bias towards the adjacent colour on the colour wheel (see page 41) which determines just how warm or cool they are. This property is worth exploiting when you are painting to create space and distance, since warm colours advance while cool ones recede.

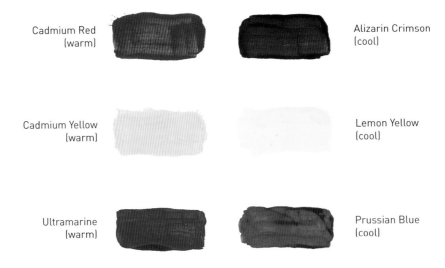

Cadmium Red
(warm)

Alizarin Crimson
(cool)

Cadmium Yellow
(warm)

Lemon Yellow
(cool)

Ultramarine
(warm)

Prussian Blue
(cool)

Prussian Blue with a
touch of Hooker's Green

Cadmium Red and
Alizarin Crimson

Hooker's Green and
Yellow Ochre

Ultramarine

PEPPERS, LEMON AND ORANGE

PALETTE USED

Lemon Yellow
Cadmium Yellow
Cadmium Orange
Cadmium Red
Alizarin Crimson
Ultramarine
Prussian Blue
Hooker's Green
Yellow Ochre
White

Hooker's Green and
Lemon Yellow

Lemon Yellow with
a touch of White

Cadmium Red and
Cadmium Orange

Cadmium Yellow and
Cadmium Orange

Secondary colours

When primary colours are mixed together they create the secondary, or complementary, colours, which are orange, violet and green. Most paint sets also contain several pre-mixed secondary colours, such as Violet, Viridian and Hooker's Green.

There are subtle differences in the secondaries produced from the warm or cool versions of each of the primaries. By understanding how to mix and use these you can influence the viewer's perception of your painting and get the exact colours you want.

Alizarin Crimson	+	Lemon Yellow	=	cool orange
Cadmium Red	+	Cadmium Yellow	=	warm orange
Ultramarine	+	Cadmium Yellow	=	warm green
Prussian Blue	+	Lemon Yellow	=	cool green
Alizarin Crimson	+	Ultramarine	=	cool violet
Cadmium Red	+	Prussian Blue	=	warm violet

GARDEN IN FROME

PALETTE USED
Lemon Yellow
Cadmium Yellow
Cadmium Red
Alizarin Crimson
Ultramarine
Prussian Blue
Burnt Sienna
Yellow Ochre
Vandyke Brown
White

Ultramarine, Yellow Ochre and White

Ultramarine and Cadmium Yellow

Cadmium Red and White with a touch of Yellow Ochre

Vandyke Brown over Cadmium Red

White and Yellow Ochre

Yellow Ochre over Lemon Yellow and Prussian Blue mix

Lemon Yellow, Prussian Blue and White

Alizarin Crimson and Lemon Yellow

Burnt Sienna

Vandyke Brown over Alizarin Crimson

Tertiary colours

A tertiary colour can also be described as an intermediary colour because it is made by mixing an approximately equal quantity of a primary colour with the secondary next to it on the colour wheel (see page 41). For example, if you combine red with violet, its neighbour to the right, you will make a red-violet, while combining red with its neighbour to the left (orange) will give you a red-orange.

You can create further intermediary colours by repeatedly mixing each neighbouring pair until you have almost continuous subtle transitions of colour. By changing the proportions of these pairings to slightly increase the bias towards one or other of the component colours, you produce even more nuanced gradations. On any section of the wheel, the run of adjacent colours forms a harmonious relationship (see pages 42–43).

As you mix these colours you will find that the infinite progression is in itself a beautiful image, giving you ideas as to how you can use these colours sensitively in your paintings.

red + violet = red-violet

red + orange = red-orange

yellow + orange = yellow-orange

yellow + green = yellow-green

blue + green = blue-green

blue + violet = blue-violet

SUMMER TABLE

PALETTE USED
Lemon Yellow
Cadmium Yellow
Cadmium Orange
Alizarin Crimson
Violet
Ultramarine
Viridian
White

Blue-violet mixed from Ultramarine and Violet and White

blue-green mixed from Ultramarine and Viridian

yellow-green mixed from Lemon Yellow and Ultramarine

Red-orange mixed from Alizarin Crimson and Cadmium Orange

Blue-violet mixed from Ultramarine and Violet

Red-violet mixed from Alizarin Crimson and Violet

Yellow-orange mixed from Cadmium Yellow and Cadmium Orange

3 COLOUR RELATIONSHIPS

Colours are always seen in relation to each other, never in isolation. To prove this to yourself, put a splash of the same colour on two pieces of paper, one white and the other tinted, and you will see immediately that they look quite different. This means that when you want to handle several colours together you will need to have an understanding of how they will react with each other and the effect the combination will have on the viewer.

The colour wheel

The traditional way to display the colour spectrum for artists is to organize the colours into a wheel, showing where they sit and the relationships between them. Understanding them in this form will help you to use colour effectively in your paintings.

On the colour wheel, the primary colours (see page 34) are positioned at equal distances apart, with each secondary colour (see page 36) between the two primaries from which it is mixed and opposite the third primary: that is to say, violet, mixed from blue and red, is opposite yellow; green, mixed from yellow and blue, is opposite red; and orange, mixed from red and yellow, is opposite blue.

Between the primary and secondary colours are the tertiary colours (see page 38), which are a subtle gradation of the mixture between the primary and the secondary: red-orange, yellow-orange, yellow-green, blue-green, blue-violet and red violet.

Although the primary colours are dissimilar to each other, they become related by the intermediary 'mixed' colours. So a painting with red and blue, which would stress the contrasting properties of those colours, could be unified by adding the intermediary red-violets and blue-violets.

As the complementaries, which sit opposite each other on the wheel (see page 48), are unlike each other, they create a strong contrast that tends to intensify both of them. If the complementaries are the same saturation (strength of colour), they can produce a very vivid effect.

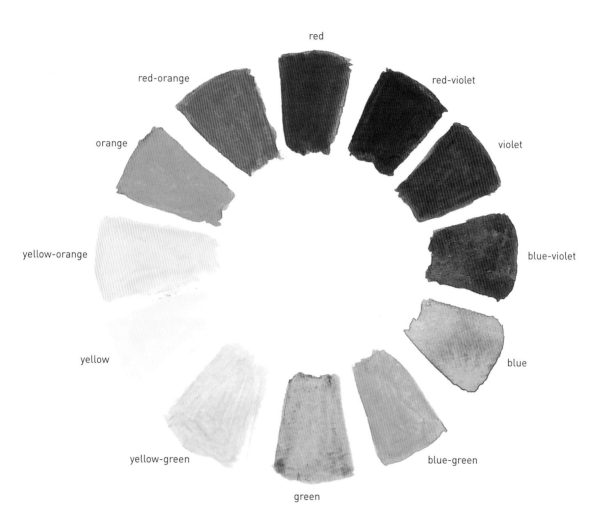

red

red-orange

orange

yellow-orange

yellow

yellow-green

green

blue-green

blue

blue-violet

violet

red-violet

Harmonious colours

Working with a range of colours that are adjacent to each other on the colour wheel – for example the range from cool blues to deep greens, or the rich transition from dark orange through red to violet, or from light green through yellow to orange – is referred to as using harmonious colour, or adjacent harmony.

Harmonious colour unifies a composition. Choosing objects for a still life that all share a colour association will make a coherent painting and while,

The family of reds ranges from very cool bluish Alizarin Crimson to orange-biased Cadmium Red.

The figs, aubergines and onions range from Ultramarine to reddish Violet.

of course, you cannot arrange the colours that exist in a landscape in the same way, as an artist you can decide which colours you will use to paint them.

The simplest harmony comes from mixing two hues then placing the resulting hue between them to create a common bond that unifies them. You can also achieve harmony by using hues of the same tonal value or saturation or applying a dominant colour that unites a range of tints and shades.

The yellow family ranges from very warm Cadmium Orange to cool Lemon Yellow.

This study of pears, peppers and parsley uses warm yellow-greens mixed from Lemon Yellow and Hooker's Green to cool Viridian.

Harmony in practice

The paintings on this page and the following pages show how using a palette of colours that are adjacent on the colour wheel brings unity and coherence to a composition. The viewer's eye understands the connections between the colours and travels round the composition, guided by the arrangement of the linked hues.

This type of harmonious colour combination is sometimes referred to as using analogous colours. With an analogous colour scheme one colour often dominates, such as yellow, a second, related colour supports, such as orange, and a third colour, which is also related to the dominant colour, provides an accent – say yellow-green.

WARM RIVER
Underpainted with a wash of well-diluted Lemon Yellow, the valley is painted with a variety of subtle mixes of Yellow Ochre, Cadmium Yellow, Burnt Sienna and Vandyke Brown. Impasto strokes of thick White and Lemon Yellow in the foreground gives perspective.

MARKET STALL
(LEFT)

The blue-green leeks
– a mix of Ultramarine
and Cadmium Yellow –
are a foil for the vivid
yellow-greens of celery
and lettuce, mixed from
Lemon Yellow and
Prussian Blue.

SUMMER FRUITS
(OPPOSITE)

Alizarin Crimson brings
harmony to the blue and
red families of colour
used in this painting. It is
mixed with Ultramarine
to create dark purple
blackberries and
blueberries and
harmonises with the
Cadmium Red of the
strawberries.

Complementary colours

Using colour with intent rather than just reproducing the colours that occur in a given scene is what makes you an artist, and understanding the position of colours on the wheel is crucial to that. The colours opposite each other on the wheel are called complementary – they complement each other and gain more brilliance by virtue of their juxtaposition – an effect used by Van Gogh, for example.

The complementary of a primary colour is always a secondary colour which is a mixture of the other two primaries. Therefore, red is complementary to green (mixed from blue and yellow); yellow is complementary to purple (mixed from blue and red); and blue is complementary to orange (mixed from yellow and red). Even a small amount of a complementary colour brings a painting to life.

Complementary red and green

Complementary blue and orange

Complementary yellow and purple

Constable often put a dash of red amid the greens of a landscape, and although it might be just a single brushmark he regarded it as playing such a strong role that he called it 'the little red soldier'.

Creating vibrancy in a composition with the use of complementary colours conveys a very different mood from the subtle effect of the harmonious colours on pages 42–47. This is called 'contrasting harmony'. Where complementaries aren't obvious you can create them by, for example, using a very yellow-green for trees and a purple-grey for the shadows; it may not be what you can actually see in nature, but it will give you a much more exciting painting. In still-life set-ups, you can deliberately choose objects in complementary colours, again exaggerating the colours to make them sing.

Cadmium
Orange

Lemon
Yellow

Alizarin
Crimson

Hooker's
Green

COMPLEMENTARY COLOUR WHEEL

Complementary colours appear opposite each other on the colour wheel.

Violet

Prussian
Blue

Complementary colour in practice

The paintings on this spread show how using a palette of colours that are opposite each other on the colour wheel – blue and orange, red and green, and yellow and purple – brings vibrancy and brilliance to a composition. It is an effect that draws the eye and demands attention.

HEALTHY BREAKFAST
(LEFT)

This still life exploits the way orange and blue work so well together. The oranges were painted with a mix of Cadmium Orange and Cadmium Yellow – adding a more intense red to the mix helps to define the shape and heighten the contrast with the Ultramarine jug. The pattern of the cloth echoes this vivid contrast.

LILIES
(LEFT)

Both warm and cool reds (Cadmium Red and Alizarin Crimson) stand out against the warm Hooker's Green foliage and cool, dense Viridian background.

THE BEACH TOWEL
(ABOVE)

The bright sand, a mixture of Cadmium Yellow and Lemon Yellow, seems even more vibrant in contrast to the violet-blue towel.

4 COLOUR PROPERTIES

If it could be definitively stated that red is always warm and blue is always cool, the use of colour would be much simpler than is the case. It's certainly true when they are placed side by side for comparison, but what's more difficult is that the temperature relies on the relationships of all the colours in a painting and on the particular reds and blues you choose.

Generally speaking, warm colours make elements in a painting advance and cool colours make them recede, so you might expect that red objects in the distance or blue ones in the foreground would destroy the three-dimensional effect you are trying to achieve. This is not necessarily so: the answer rests in the colour mixtures you use.

On the colour wheel on page 41, you can see that each primary colour has a cool colour at one side and a warm one at the other. Cadmium Red sits towards yellow and so is warmer than Alizarin Crimson, which is towards blue. Cadmium Yellow has orange in it and is therefore warmer than Lemon Yellow, which has green and a touch of blue in it. Prussian Blue is cool in comparison to Ultramarine, which has a touch of red.

The clearest purple comes from a mix of Ultramarine and Alizarin Crimson. If you mix Cadmium Red with either of the blues you will get a muted purple bordering on grey. The reason for this is that Cadmium Red has that bit of yellow, so in fact you are mixing the three primaries. That subtle mix of colour, called neutralized, is extremely useful for painting shadows.

Knowing the potential mixes to use will make your pictures both more exciting to paint and to look at; you'll have the satisfaction of knowing that your considered choices have created an effect. Always work with the colours rather than trying to push them to do what they cannot. Practise the mixes systematically before you embark on a painting, but be open to surprises too, since they are exciting in themselves and will teach you something new every time you use them.

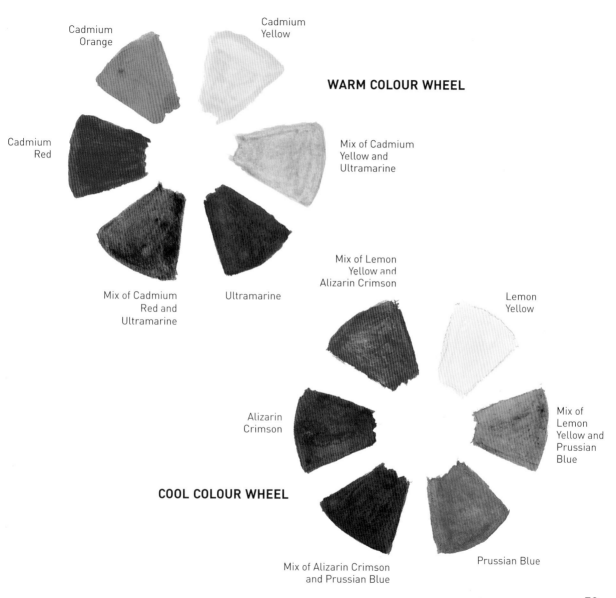

Cadmium
Orange

Cadmium
Yellow

WARM COLOUR WHEEL

Cadmium
Red

Mix of Cadmium
Yellow and
Ultramarine

Mix of Cadmium
Red and
Ultramarine

Ultramarine

Mix of Lemon
Yellow and
Alizarin Crimson

Lemon
Yellow

Mix of
Lemon
Yellow and
Prussian
Blue

Alizarin
Crimson

COOL COLOUR WHEEL

Prussian Blue

Mix of Alizarin Crimson
and Prussian Blue

Warm and cool colours in practice

As you discovered on pages 52–53, it's possible to mix warm and cool versions of secondary colours by the clever use of warm and cool primaries. Using colour temperature in your paintings, working on the basis that warm colours advance and cool ones recede, you can give a feeling of depth even while using the same colour – for example, a landscape with wheat fields in the foreground and in the distance would use warm Cadmium Yellow for the former and washed out, cool Lemon Yellow for the latter. Colour temperature also allows you to convey the physical temperature of a scene so that the viewer can understand the season without signifiers such as bare trees or flowers in bloom.

Shadows are clearly cool, and in the painting shown opposite the New York urban landscape has strong, greeny, cool shadows set against areas where the light hits the side of the building, painted in a warm creamy yellow. The technique of painting used here was a series of scumbled and overlaid colours to produce mixes that are not flat. You can see the underlayer showing through, particularly in the shadow parts where I have used green over red as a complementary contrast. I steered clear of neutral colours to achieve a dramatic winter's day.

In the painting of Hampstead Heath in London on pages 56–57, the shadows are also cool but brighter. This was a warm day, so the chosen warm and cool colours are more simply put down with less mixing and more straightforward, clear brushstrokes. The warm colours are a creamy orangey yellow while the colours in the shadows are a cool blue, with the dark foliage a mixture of green and red to make a dark, intense green. Interestingly, the warm and cool colours are from the same mixes in both paintings but applied using different techniques for a completely different overall effect.

It is interesting to compare the paintings of such different locations and seasons – the buildings are austere and are rendered with linear brushstrokes, while the landscape is soft and natural, so curvy, broken, looser marks of clear colour were appropriate.

Viridian overlaying Alizarin Crimson

White overlaying Alizarin Crimson

Lemon Yellow and White

Glazes of Yellow Ochre and Black

NEW YORK IN WINTER

PALETTE USED
Lemon Yellow
Alizarin Crimson
Prussian Blue
Viridian
Burnt Sienna
Yellow Ochre
Black
White

Glazes of Alizarin Crimson and White over Black

Prussian Blue and Viridian scumbled with Alizarin Crimson

Burnt Sienna

Prussian Blue, Alizarin Crimson, White and Lemon Yellow brushstrokes

HAMPSTEAD HEATH

The warm and cool colours in this painting use the same mixes as on the previous page, but the different techniques employed create a completely different effect.

5 MIXING COLOUR

As you learnt on pages 8–9, there are two ways to physically mix the colours you want from your set of acrylic paints. Just as you should make deliberate choices about the colours that you use, the method of mixing and applying them is another decision to take since each has its particular quality.

Palette mixing

Mixing pigments in a palette and then applying the mix to the paper enables you to create a subtle range of colours as you can play with the proportions of each pigment before beginning to paint. While this may be slow going at first, with practice you'll quickly be able to achieve the effect you want.

Overlaying

Allowing a colour to dry on the paper and then overlaying it with another colour is a particularly useful technique to use if you want to make an area stand out from the rest of the painting as it creates a brilliance of colour. You can also create a shadow very effectively by overlaying a colour to make it appear darker.

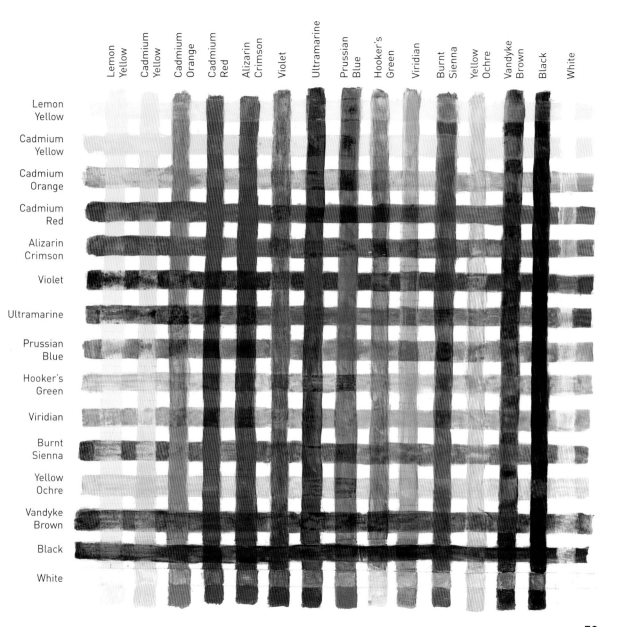

Lemon Yellow · Cadmium Yellow · Cadmium Orange · Cadmium Red · Alizarin Crimson · Violet · Ultramarine · Prussian Blue · Hooker's Green · Viridian · Burnt Sienna · Yellow Ochre · Vandyke Brown · Black · White

Lemon Yellow
Cadmium Yellow
Cadmium Orange
Cadmium Red
Alizarin Crimson
Violet
Ultramarine
Prussian Blue
Hooker's Green
Viridian
Burnt Sienna
Yellow Ochre
Vandyke Brown
Black
White

Palette mixes

LEMON YELLOW

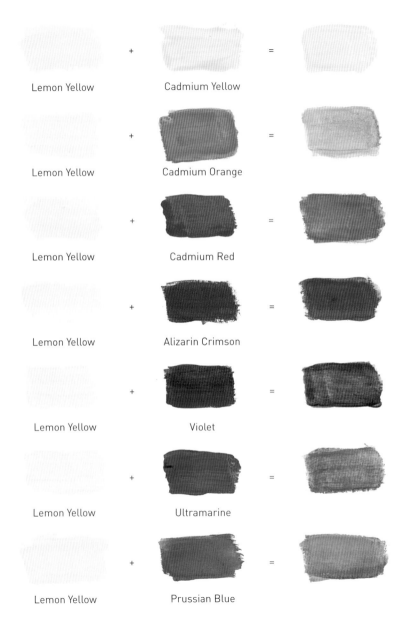

Lemon Yellow	+ Cadmium Yellow	=
Lemon Yellow	+ Cadmium Orange	=
Lemon Yellow	+ Cadmium Red	=
Lemon Yellow	+ Alizarin Crimson	=
Lemon Yellow	+ Violet	=
Lemon Yellow	+ Ultramarine	=
Lemon Yellow	+ Prussian Blue	=

Lemon Yellow + Hooker's Green =

Lemon Yellow + Viridian =

Lemon Yellow + Burnt Sienna =

Lemon Yellow + Yellow Ochre =

Lemon Yellow + Vandyke Brown =

Lemon Yellow + Black =

Lemon Yellow + White =

CADMIUM YELLOW

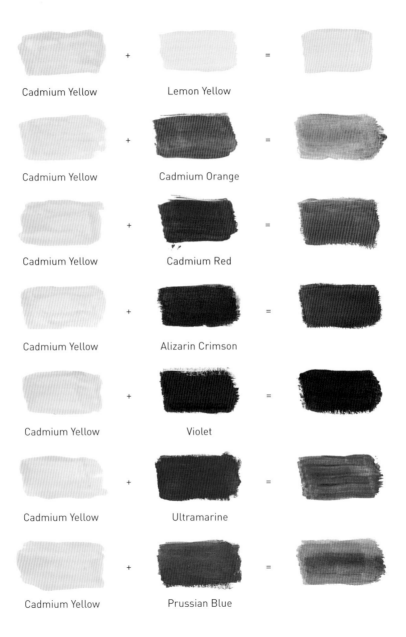

Cadmium Yellow + Lemon Yellow =

Cadmium Yellow + Cadmium Orange =

Cadmium Yellow + Cadmium Red =

Cadmium Yellow + Alizarin Crimson =

Cadmium Yellow + Violet =

Cadmium Yellow + Ultramarine =

Cadmium Yellow + Prussian Blue =

Cadmium Yellow	+	Hooker's Green	=	
Cadmium Yellow	+	Viridian	=	
Cadmium Yellow	+	Burnt Sienna	=	
Cadmium Yellow	+	Yellow Ochre	=	
Cadmium Yellow	+	Vandyke Brown	=	
Cadmium Yellow	+	Black	=	
Cadmium Yellow	+	White	=	

Palette mixing in practice

Alizarin Crimson mixed with Yellow Ochre and a touch of Black

Cadmium Yellow and Lemon Yellow

Yellow Ochre with a touch of Cadmium Red

White, Ultramarine and Alizarin Crimson

Cadmium Yellow over a mix of Lemon Yellow and Viridian

Black and White mixed with Ultramarine

CANTALOUPE

PALETTE USED

Lemon Yellow
Cadmium Yellow
Cadmium Red
Alizarin Crimson
Ultramarine
Viridian
Yellow Ochre
Black
White

The tablecloth, a graded palette mix of Cadmium Yellow, Lemon Yellow and White, sets the tone and colour of this painting. The dark creases are emphasised with a darker yellow mix and the lighter areas with more White where the light hits the edges. Viridian was used for the pattern, and was mixed in the palette with Prussian Blue for the shadowed areas and with Cadmium Yellow and White for the areas flooded with light. Elsewhere, Cadmium Red was also used, and again was mixed in the palette with White and yellow for the areas where the light hits the pattern.

CADMIUM ORANGE

Cadmium Orange	+	Lemon Yellow	=
Cadmium Orange	+	Cadmium Yellow	=
Cadmium Orange	+	Cadmium Red	=
Cadmium Orange	+	Alizarin Crimson	=
Cadmium Orange	+	Violet	=
Cadmium Orange	+	Ultramarine	=
Cadmium Orange	+	Prussian Blue	=

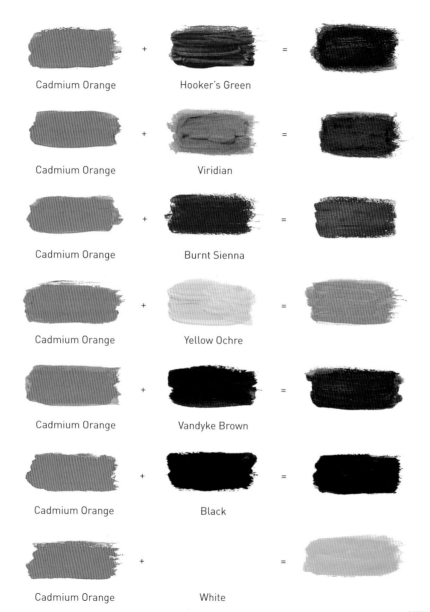

Cadmium Orange + Hooker's Green =

Cadmium Orange + Viridian =

Cadmium Orange + Burnt Sienna =

Cadmium Orange + Yellow Ochre =

Cadmium Orange + Vandyke Brown =

Cadmium Orange + Black =

Cadmium Orange + White =

CADMIUM RED

Cadmium Red + Lemon Yellow =

Cadmium Red + Cadmium Yellow =

Cadmium Red + Cadmium Orange =

Cadmium Red + Alizarin Crimson =

Cadmium Red + Violet =

Cadmium Red + Ultramarine =

Cadmium Red + Prussian Blue =

Cadmium Red + Hooker's Green =

Cadmium Red + Viridian =

Cadmium Red + Burnt Sienna =

Cadmium Red + Yellow Ochre =

Cadmium Red + Vandyke Brown =

Cadmium Red + Black =

Cadmium Red + White =

ALIZARIN CRIMSON

Alizarin Crimson	+	Lemon Yellow	=
Alizarin Crimson	+	Cadmium Yellow	=
Alizarin Crimson	+	Cadmium Orange	=
Alizarin Crimson	+	Cadmium Red	=
Alizarin Crimson	+	Violet	=
Alizarin Crimson	+	Ultramarine	=
Alizarin Crimson	+	Prussian Blue	=

Alizarin Crimson	+ Hooker's Green	=
Alizarin Crimson	+ Viridian	=
Alizarin Crimson	+ Burnt Sienna	=
Alizarin Crimson	+ Yellow Ochre	=
Alizarin Crimson	+ Vandyke Brown	=
Alizarin Crimson	+ Black	=
Alizarin Crimson	+ White	=

Palette mixing in practice

Poppies are a wonderful subject for experimenting with shades of red. Cadmium Red was mixed in the palette with a variety of different colours, including Alizarin Crimson, White and Cadmium Orange, to create a range of vivid reds and pinks. These palette mixes were used to paint layers of thick bright colour, one over another. As acrylics dry quickly, the petals were painted swiftly to allow the colours to blend, White blurring into pink and Cadmium Orange loosely applied to emphasise the outer petals spreading open. The background was painted in streaks of Ultramarine, White and Black, broken up with green-yellow, pink and white, which were mixed in a palette before being applied.

Cadmium Red and
Alizarin Crimson

Alizarin Crimson
and a touch of Black

Alizarin Crimson scumbled
over a mixture of White and
Cadmium Red

POPPIES

PALETTE USED
Cadmium Red
Cadmium Orange
Alizarin Crimson
Ultramarine
Black
White

Cadmium Orange
and Cadmium Red

Alizarin Crimson, Cadmium Red
and a touch of Ultramarine

White and Alizarin
Crimson

VIOLET

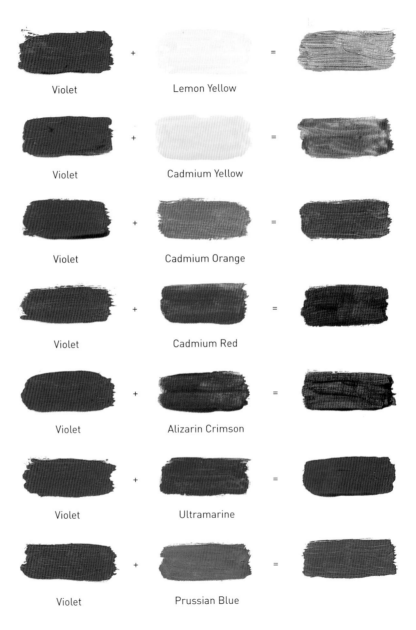

Violet + Lemon Yellow =

Violet + Cadmium Yellow =

Violet + Cadmium Orange =

Violet + Cadmium Red =

Violet + Alizarin Crimson =

Violet + Ultramarine =

Violet + Prussian Blue =

Violet + Hooker's Green =

Violet + Viridian =

Violet + Burnt Sienna =

Violet + Yellow Ochre =

Violet + Vandyke Brown =

Violet + Black =

Violet + White =

ULTRAMARINE

Ultramarine + Lemon Yellow =

Ultramarine + Cadmium Yellow =

Ultramarine + Cadmium Orange =

Ultramarine + Cadmium Red =

Ultramarine + Alizarin Crimson =

Ultramarine + Violet =

Ultramarine + Prussian Blue =

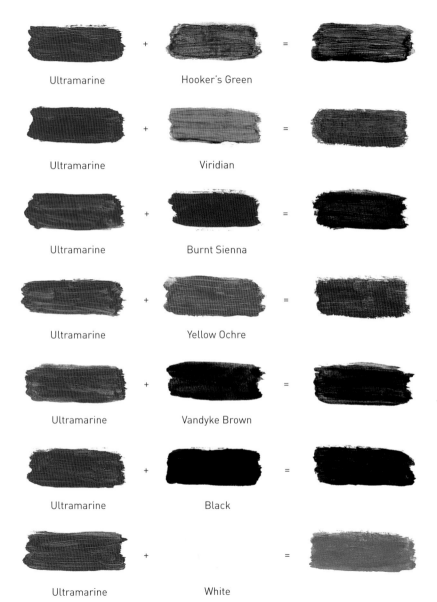

Ultramarine + Hooker's Green =

Ultramarine + Viridian =

Ultramarine + Burnt Sienna =

Ultramarine + Yellow Ochre =

Ultramarine + Vandyke Brown =

Ultramarine + Black =

Ultramarine + White =

PRUSSIAN BLUE

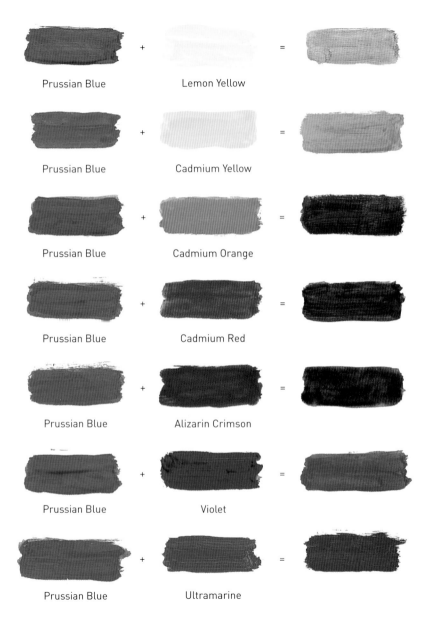

Prussian Blue + Lemon Yellow =

Prussian Blue + Cadmium Yellow =

Prussian Blue + Cadmium Orange =

Prussian Blue + Cadmium Red =

Prussian Blue + Alizarin Crimson =

Prussian Blue + Violet =

Prussian Blue + Ultramarine =

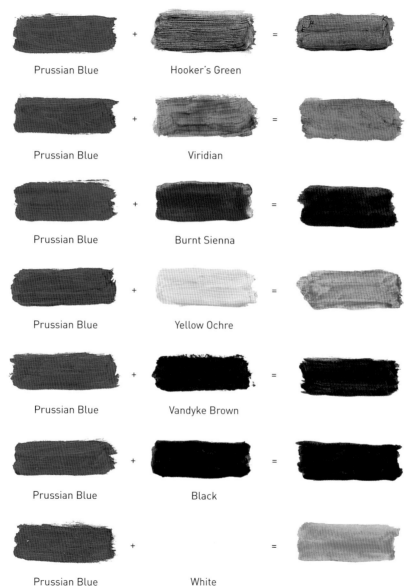

Prussian Blue + Hooker's Green =

Prussian Blue + Viridian =

Prussian Blue + Burnt Sienna =

Prussian Blue + Yellow Ochre =

Prussian Blue + Vandyke Brown =

Prussian Blue + Black =

Prussian Blue + White =

Palette mixing in practice

WINDY SKY

PALETTE USED

Cadmium Red

Alizarin Crimson

Ultramarine

Prussian Blue

Hooker's Green

Yellow Ochre

Black

White

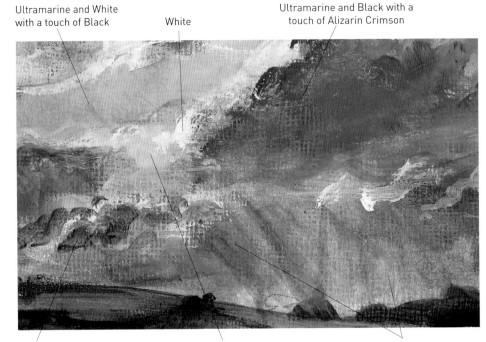

Ultramarine and White with a touch of Black

White

Ultramarine and Black with a touch of Alizarin Crimson

Black, Alizarin Crimson and a Yellow Ochre mix

Yellow Ochre

Black and Hooker's Green mix with a little Prussian Blue

An initial palette mix of Black and Ultramarine was thinned and diluted to paint the clouds before thicker, palette-mixed paint was brushed on in swoops and whirls. Similarly, the fields were painted in a palette mix of Hooker's Green, Prussian Blue and a touch of Black for the distant hills with a Cadmium Red, Black and Yellow Ochre mix for the furrowed hill, before adding directional brushmarks. Finally the blues of the sky were carefully marked out with a mix of Ultramarine and White. The clouds were edged with pure White and threaded through with touches of Yellow Ochre highlighted with white.

HOOKER'S GREEN

Hooker's Green + Lemon Yellow =

Hooker's Green + Cadmium Yellow =

Hooker's Green + Cadmium Orange =

Hooker's Green + Cadmium Red =

Hooker's Green + Alizarin Crimson =

Hooker's Green + Violet =

Hooker's Green + Ultramarine =

Hooker's Green + Prussian Blue =

Hooker's Green + Viridian =

Hooker's Green + Burnt Sienna =

Hooker's Green + Yellow Ochre =

Hooker's Green + Vandyke Brown =

Hooker's Green + Black =

Hooker's Green + White =

VIRIDIAN

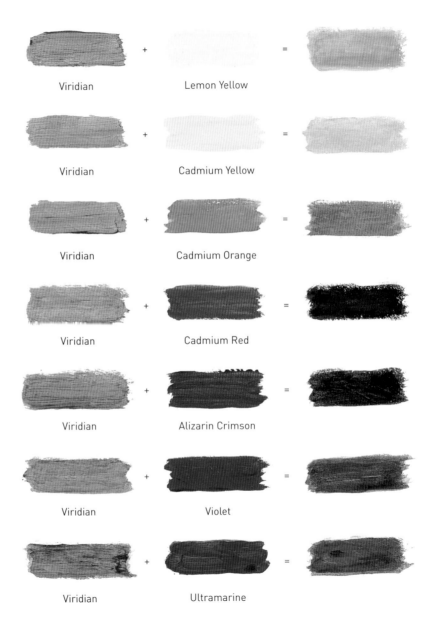

Viridian + Lemon Yellow =

Viridian + Cadmium Yellow =

Viridian + Cadmium Orange =

Viridian + Cadmium Red =

Viridian + Alizarin Crimson =

Viridian + Violet =

Viridian + Ultramarine =

Viridian + Prussian Blue =

Viridian + Hooker's Green =

Viridian + Burnt Sienna =

Viridian + Yellow Ochre =

Viridian + Vandyke Brown =

Viridian + Black =

Viridian + White =

BURNT SIENNA

Burnt Sienna + Lemon Yellow =

Burnt Sienna + Cadmium Yellow =

Burnt Sienna + Cadmium Orange =

Burnt Sienna + Cadmium Red =

Burnt Sienna + Alizarin Crimson =

Burnt Sienna + Violet =

Burnt Sienna + Ultramarine =

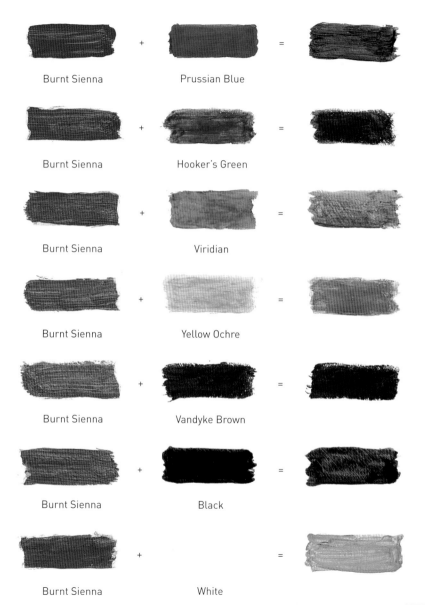

Burnt Sienna + Prussian Blue =

Burnt Sienna + Hooker's Green =

Burnt Sienna + Viridian =

Burnt Sienna + Yellow Ochre =

Burnt Sienna + Vandyke Brown =

Burnt Sienna + Black =

Burnt Sienna + White =

Palette mixing in practice

TUSCAN UMBRELLA PINES

PALETTE USED

Cadmium Yellow

Alizarin Crimson

Prussian Blue

Viridian

Burnt Sienna

Yellow Ochre

Black

White

Viridian, Prussian Blue and Black

Yellow Ochre and Cadmium Yellow

Burnt Sienna and Alizarin Crimson

Viridian, Prussian Blue and Black

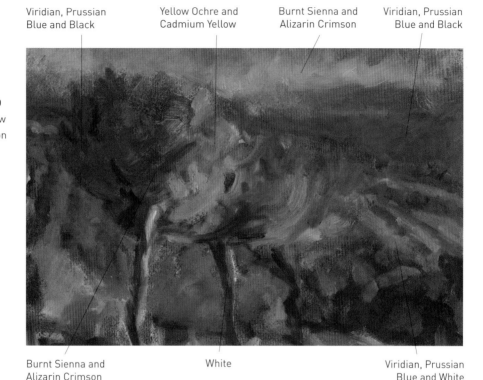

Burnt Sienna and Alizarin Crimson

White

Viridian, Prussian Blue and White

A palette mix of Burnt Sienna and Alizarin Crimson covers the whole support of the painting as a primer, with the acrylics applied quite loosely over the top. Spaces were left around the tree shapes and landscape to allow the lovely warm glow of the palette mix to shine through the brushstrokes.

Other mixes include Yellow Ochre and Cadmium Yellow that are blended a little into the darker green trees, which are also a palette mix of Prussian Blue, Black and Viridian. White was used to lighten the sun-kissed areas slightly and reinforce the sense a warm, late-summer evening.

YELLOW OCHRE

Yellow Ochre   +   Lemon Yellow   =

Yellow Ochre   +   Cadmium Yellow   =

Yellow Ochre   +   Cadmium Orange   =

Yellow Ochre   +   Cadmium Red   =

Yellow Ochre   +   Alizarin Crimson   =

Yellow Ochre   +   Violet   =

Yellow Ochre   +   Ultramarine   =

Yellow Ochre   +   Prussian Blue   =

Yellow Ochre   +   Hooker's Green   =

Yellow Ochre   +   Viridian   =

Yellow Ochre   +   Burnt Sienna   =

Yellow Ochre   +   Vandyke Brown   =

Yellow Ochre   +   Black   =

Yellow Ochre   +   White   =

VANDYKE BROWN

Vandyke Brown + Lemon Yellow =

Vandyke Brown + Cadmium Yellow =

Vandyke Brown + Cadmium Orange =

Vandyke Brown + Cadmium Red =

Vandyke Brown + Alizarin Crimson =

Vandyke Brown + Violet =

Vandyke Brown + Ultramarine =

Vandyke Brown + Prussian Blue =

Vandyke Brown + Hooker's Green =

Vandyke Brown + Viridian =

Vandyke Brown + Burnt Sienna =

Vandyke Brown + Yellow Ochre =

Vandyke Brown + Black =

Vandyke Brown + White =

BLACK

Black + Lemon Yellow =

Black + Cadmium Yellow =

Black + Cadmium Orange =

Black + Cadmium Red =

Black + Alizarin Crimson =

Black + Violet =

Black + Ultramarine =

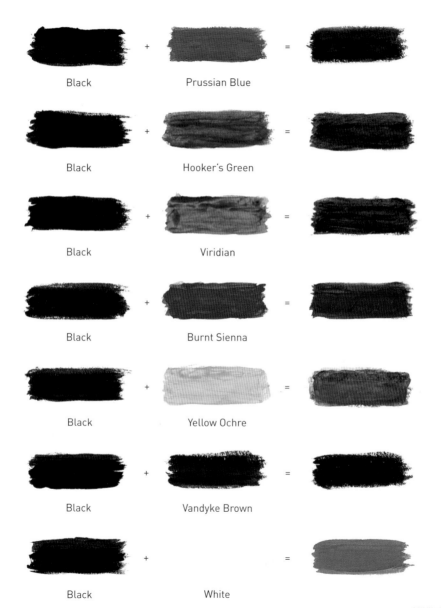

Black   +   Prussian Blue   =

Black   +   Hooker's Green   =

Black   +   Viridian   =

Black   +   Burnt Sienna   =

Black   +   Yellow Ochre   =

Black   +   Vandyke Brown   =

Black   +   White   =

Palette mixing in practice

Using Black paint directly from the tube is often too harsh and will not provide the subtle shades needed for shape and form. By mixing a slightly diluted Black with another colour you can achieve interesting darks that work well for deep shadows. This painting has a Viridian-green bias, which is very cool, and so the shadows were given a slightly warmer bias. Violet and Alizarin Crimson were mixed in the palette with Black to give depth and luminosity to a shape that would otherwise be a hard, opaque black mark. The leaves of the palm trees were a palette mix of Ultramarine and Viridian.

Black, Ultramarine and Viridian

Prussian Blue

Lemon Yellow, White and Prussian Blue

Black, Violet and Alizarin Crimson

White and Prussian Blue

SUNSET BOULEVARD

PALETTE USED

Lemon Yellow
Alizarin Crimson
Violet
Ultramarine
Prussian Blue
Viridian
Black
White

WHITE

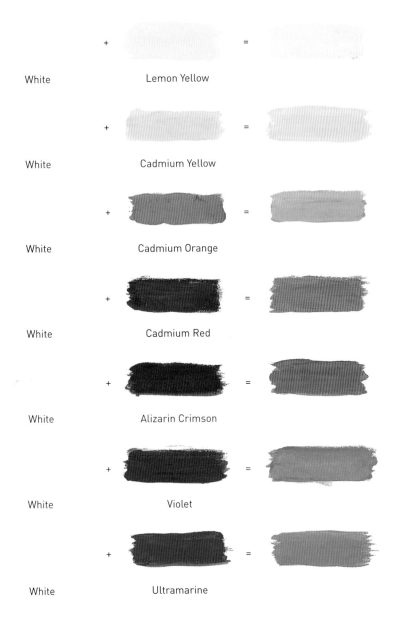

White + Lemon Yellow =

White + Cadmium Yellow =

White + Cadmium Orange =

White + Cadmium Red =

White + Alizarin Crimson =

White + Violet =

White + Ultramarine =

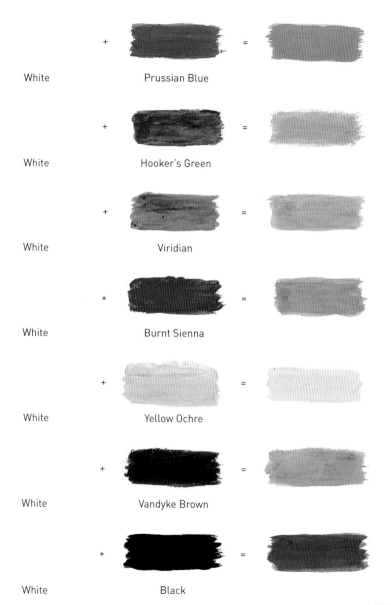

White   +   Prussian Blue   =

White   +   Hooker's Green   =

White   +   Viridian   =

White   +   Burnt Sienna   =

White   +   Yellow Ochre   =

White   +   Vandyke Brown   =

White   +   Black   =

Overlaying

LEMON YELLOW

Lemon Yellow + Cadmium Yellow

Lemon Yellow + Cadmium Orange

Lemon Yellow + Ultramarine

Lemon Yellow + Prussian Blue

Lemon Yellow + Yellow Ochre

Lemon Yellow + Vandyke Brown

Lemon Yellow + Cadmium Red

Lemon Yellow + Alizarin Crimson

Lemon Yellow + Violet

Lemon Yellow + Hooker's Green

Lemon Yellow + Viridian

Lemon Yellow + Burnt Sienna

Lemon Yellow + Black

Lemon Yellow + White

CADMIUM YELLOW

Cadmium Yellow + Lemon Yellow

Cadmium Yellow + Cadmium Orange

Cadmium Yellow + Ultramarine

Cadmium Yellow + Prussian Blue

Cadmium Yellow + Yellow Ochre

Cadmium Yellow + Vandyke Brown

Cadmium Yellow + Cadmium Red

Cadmium Yellow + Alizarin Crimson

Cadmium Yellow + Violet

Cadmium Yellow + Hooker's Green

Cadmium Yellow + Viridian

Cadmium Yellow + Burnt Sienna

Cadmium Yellow + Black

Cadmium Yellow + White

CADMIUM ORANGE

Cadmium Orange + Lemon Yellow

Cadmium Orange + Cadmium Yellow

Cadmium Orange + Ultramarine

Cadmium Orange + Prussian Blue

Cadmium Orange + Yellow Ochre

Cadmium Orange + Vandyke Brown

Cadmium Orange + Cadmium Red

Cadmium Orange + Alizarin Crimson

Cadmium Orange + Violet

Cadmium Orange + Hooker's Green

Cadmium Orange + Viridian

Cadmium Orange + Burnt Sienna

Cadmium Orange + Black

Cadmium Orange + White

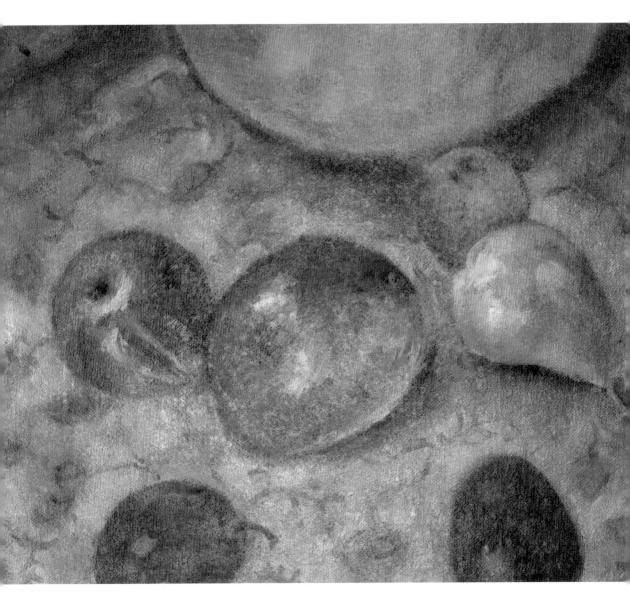

Overlaying in practice

Cadmium Orange and
Alizarin Crimson glaze

Alizarin Crimson
and Violet glaze

Cadmium Orange and
Alizarin Crimson glaze

**MANGO AND
GREEN BOWL**

PALETTE USED

Lemon Yellow
Cadmium Orange
Cadmium Red
Alizarin Crimson
Violet
White

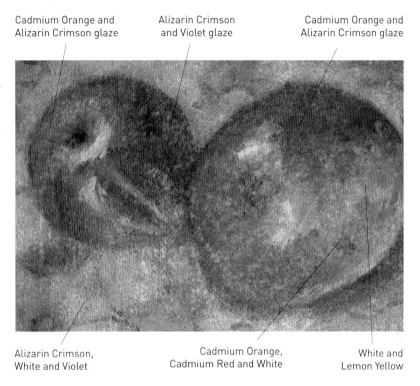

Alizarin Crimson,
White and Violet

Cadmium Orange,
Cadmium Red and White

White and
Lemon Yellow

Overlaying is a useful technique to achieve that variety of texture and gradations of colour that fruit often has. The base colour will affect the colour laid on top, and so on with subsequent glazes, while the slight transparency exploits the sheen of fruit. In this painting, the mango was painted with several colours, starting with a mixture of Cadmium Orange and Cadmium Red with a touch of White. This was glazed with further layers of Cadmium Orange, Alizarin Crimson, Lemon Yellow and Violet. Finally the lightest part of the fruit was painted with White and Lemon Yellow to give shape and form. This overlaying never completely obscured the base colour of Alizarin Crimson used for the cloth.

CADMIUM RED

Cadmium Red + Lemon Yellow

Cadmium Red + Cadmium Yellow

Cadmium Red + Ultramarine

Cadmium Red + Prussian Blue

Cadmium Red + Yellow Ochre

Cadmium Red + Vandyke Brown

Cadmium Red + Cadmium Orange

Cadmium Red + Alizarin Crimson

Cadmium Red + Violet

Cadmium Red + Hooker's Green

Cadmium Red + Viridian

Cadmium Red + Burnt Sienna

Cadmium Red + Black

Cadmium Red + White

ALIZARIN CRIMSON

Alizarin Crimson + Lemon Yellow

Alizarin Crimson + Cadmium Yellow

Alizarin Crimson + Ultramarine

Alizarin Crimson + Prussian Blue

Alizarin Crimson + Yellow Ochre

Alizarin Crimson + Vandyke Brown

Alizarin Crimson + Cadmium Orange

Alizarin Crimson + Cadmium Red

Alizarin Crimson + Violet

Alizarin Crimson + Hooker's Green

Alizarin Crimson + Viridian

Alizarin Crimson + Burnt Sienna

Alizarin Crimson + Black

Alizarin Crimson + White

VIOLET

Violet + Lemon Yellow

Violet + Cadmium Yellow

Violet + Ultramarine

Violet + Prussian Blue

Violet + Yellow Ochre

Violet + Vandyke Brown

Violet + Cadmium Orange

Violet + Cadmium Red

Violet + Alizarin Crimson

Violet + Hooker's Green

Violet + Viridian

Violet + Burnt Sienna

Violet + Black

Violet + White

Overlaying in practice

Alizarin Crimson
and White glaze

Violet and
Ultramarine glaze

Cadmium Orange
over Black

Ultramarine and Black
over Alizarin Crimson
and White

Viridian with
Yellow Ochre and
White glaze

Black over Ultramarine
and Violet glaze

Cadmium Yellow and
Ultramarine over Black

Violet, Alizarin
Crimson and
White glaze

**SHADOWED
STILL LIFE**

PALETTE USED

Cadmium Yellow

Cadmium Orange

Alizarin Crimson

Violet

Ultramarine

Viridian

Yellow Ochre

Black

White

The strong shadows and angular shapes of this cubist-style painting provide an excellent example of overlaying techniques. Instead of blending the colours, they are overlaid very sharply one area against another, as shown in the area around the jug and the triangular bowl. The watercolour background was Violet and Ultramarine with Alizarin Crimson and White dabbled over it. The strong shadows from the twigs were overlaid in a different blue. The glass and bottle were loosely painted over the blue as if the shadows pass over only part of the vessels.

ULTRAMARINE

Ultramarine + Lemon Yellow

Ultramarine + Cadmium Yellow

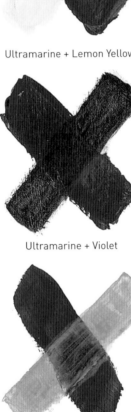

Ultramarine + Violet

Ultramarine + Prussian Blue

Ultramarine + Yellow Ochre

Ultramarine + Vandyke Brown

Ultramarine + Cadmium Orange

Ultramarine + Cadmium Red

Ultramarine + Alizarin Crimson

Ultramarine + Hooker's Green

Ultramarine + Viridian

Ultramarine + Burnt Sienna

Ultramarine + Black

Ultramarine + White

PRUSSIAN BLUE

Prussian Blue + Lemon Yellow

Prussian Blue + Cadmium Yellow

Prussian Blue + Violet

Prussian Blue + Ultramarine

Prussian Blue + Yellow Ochre

Prussian Blue + Vandyke Brown

Prussian Blue + Cadmium Orange

Prussian Blue + Cadmium Red

Prussian Blue + Alizarin Crimson

Prussian Blue + Hooker's Green

Prussian Blue + Viridian

Prussian Blue + Burnt Sienna

Prussian Blue + Black

Prussian Blue + White

HOOKER'S GREEN

Hooker's Green + Lemon Yellow

Hooker's Green + Cadmium Yellow

Hooker's Green + Violet

Hooker's Green + Ultramarine

Hooker's Green + Yellow Ochre

Hooker's Green + Vandyke Brown

Hooker's Green + Cadmium Orange

Hooker's Green + Cadmium Red

Hooker's Green + Alizarin Crimson

Hooker's Green + Prussian Blue

Hooker's Green + Viridian

Hooker's Green + Burnt Sienna

Hooker's Green + Black

Hooker's Green + White

Overlaying in practice

Hooker's Green
over Ultramarine

White over
Burnt Sienna

Alizarin Crimson
over Violet

**RECLINING
NUDE**

PALETTE USED

Lemon Yellow
Alizarin Crimson
Violet
Ultramarine
Hooker's Green
Burnt Sienna
White

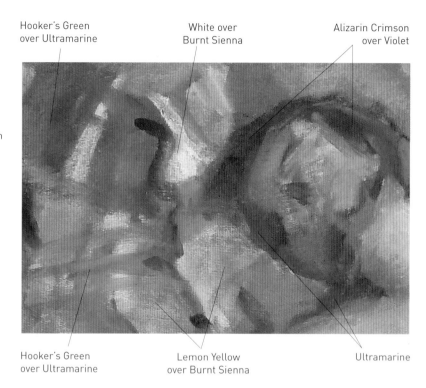

Hooker's Green
over Ultramarine

Lemon Yellow
over Burnt Sienna

Ultramarine

The way the colours are layered one over the other in this nude emphasises the shadows and curves of the limbs and helps to make the form of the body more solid. The base colour of the body is a cool Lemon Yellow but a thin overlay of Hooker's Green provides the shadows over the thighs and stomach. Strokes of Burnt Sienna overlay Lemon Yellow where the light hits the edges of the body to highlight the curve. The face was left undetailed but the shadow of the neck against the cloth was created using a thin layer of Ultramarine. The cloth echoes the green shadows of the body, with mixes of Hooker's Green and Lemon Yellow laid in glazes on top of Burnt Sienna watercolour.

VIRIDIAN

Viridian + Lemon Yellow

Viridian + Cadmium Yellow

Viridian + Violet

Viridian + Ultramarine

Viridian + Yellow Ochre

Viridian + Vandyke Brown

Viridian + Cadmium Orange

Viridian + Cadmium Red

Viridian + Alizarin Crimson

Viridian + Prussian Blue

Viridian + Hooker's Green

Viridian + Burnt Sienna

Viridian + Black

Viridian + White

BURNT SIENNA

Burnt Sienna + Lemon Yellow

Burnt Sienna + Cadmium Yellow

Burnt Sienna + Violet

Burnt Sienna + Ultramarine

Burnt Sienna + Yellow Ochre

Burnt Sienna + Vandyke Brown

Burnt Sienna + Cadmium Orange

Burnt Sienna + Cadmium Red

Burnt Sienna + Alizarin Crimson

Burnt Sienna + Prussian Blue

Burnt Sienna + Hooker's Green

Burnt Sienna + Viridian

Burnt Sienna + Black

Burnt Sienna + White

YELLOW OCHRE

Yellow Ochre + Lemon Yellow

Yellow Ochre + Cadmium Yellow

Yellow Ochre + Violet

Yellow Ochre + Ultramarine

Yellow Ochre + Burnt Sienna

Yellow Ochre + Vandyke Brown

Yellow Ochre + Cadmium Orange

Yellow Ochre + Cadmium Red

Yellow Ochre + Alizarin Crimson

Yellow Ochre + Prussian Blue

Yellow Ochre + Hooker's Green

Yellow Ochre + Viridian

Yellow Ochre + Black

Yellow Ochre + White

Overlaying in practice

The cloth was painted in Yellow Ochre and overlaid with scumbled Cadmium Orange in the foreground. Cadmium Red layers were added in the centre and top and then the left-hand corner was overlaid with another layer of Yellow Ochre. The Prussian Blue bowl and vase were overlaid with Ultramarine for the darker areas and a White and blue layer for the lighter areas. The artichoke is composed of curved brushmarks including Vandyke Brown, Lemon Yellow and Burnt Sienna. Yellow Ochre can be seen through all the layers of colour in the painting and brings a sense of harmony to the whole composition.

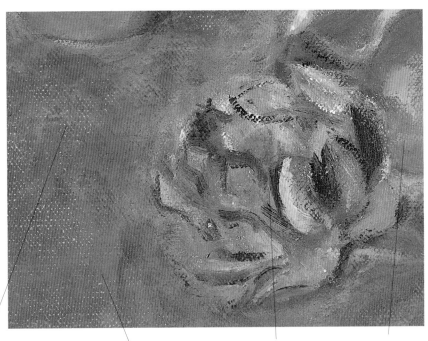

DRIED FLOWERS

PALETTE USED
Lemon Yellow
Cadmium Orange
Cadmium Red
Prussian Blue
Burnt Sienna
Yellow Ochre

Cadmium Red over Cadmium Orange and Yellow Ochre

Cadmium Orange over Yellow Ochre

Burnt Sienna over Lemon Yellow and Yellow Ochre

Prussian Blue over Lemon Yellow and Yellow Ochre

VANDYKE BROWN

Vandyke Brown + Lemon Yellow

Vandyke Brown + Cadmium Yellow

Vandyke Brown + Violet

Vandyke Brown + Ultramarine

Vandyke Brown + Burnt Sienna

Vandyke Brown + Yellow Ochre

Vandyke Brown + Cadmium Orange

Vandyke Brown + Cadmium Red

Vandyke Brown + Alizarin Crimson

Vandyke Brown + Prussian Blue

Vandyke Brown + Hooker's Green

Vandyke Brown + Viridian

Vandyke Brown + Black

Vandyke Brown + White

BLACK

Black + Lemon Yellow

Black + Cadmium Yellow

Black + Violet

Black + Ultramarine

Black + Burnt Sienna

Black + Yellow Ochre

Black + Cadmium Orange

Black + Cadmium Red

Black + Alizarin Crimson

Black + Prussian Blue

Black + Hooker's Green

Black + Viridian

Black + Vandyke Brown

Black + White

WHITE

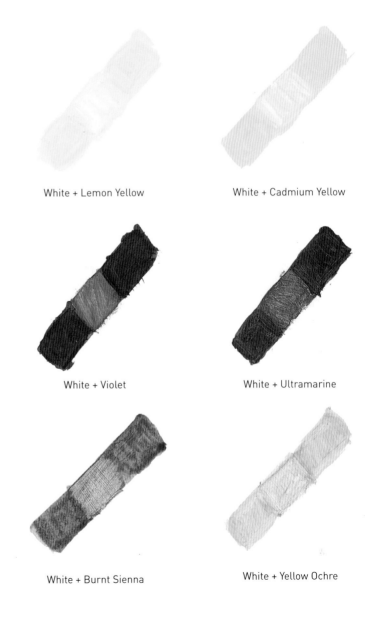

White + Lemon Yellow

White + Cadmium Yellow

White + Violet

White + Ultramarine

White + Burnt Sienna

White + Yellow Ochre

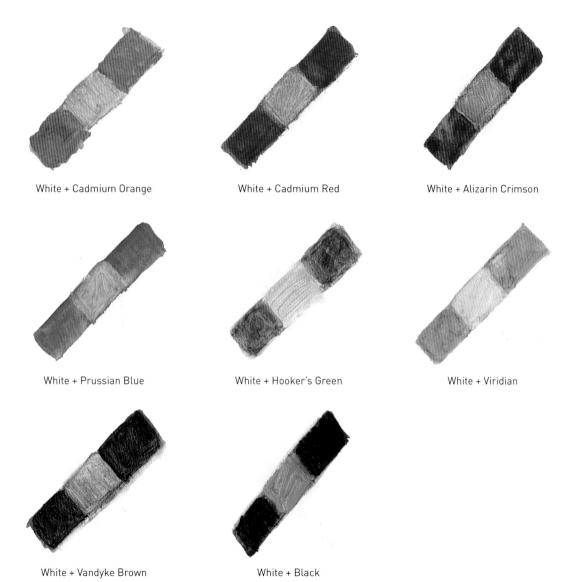

White + Cadmium Orange

White + Cadmium Red

White + Alizarin Crimson

White + Prussian Blue

White + Hooker's Green

White + Viridian

White + Vandyke Brown

White + Black

Overlaying in practice

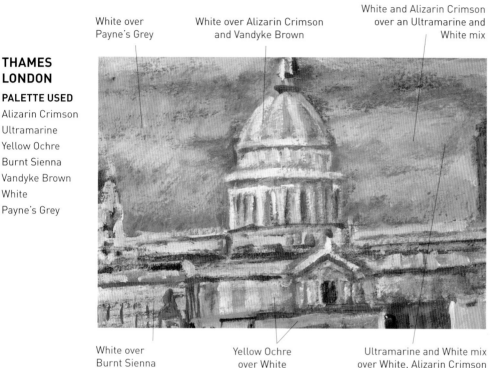

White over
Payne's Grey

White over Alizarin Crimson
and Vandyke Brown

White and Alizarin Crimson
over an Ultramarine and
White mix

**THAMES
LONDON**

PALETTE USED

Alizarin Crimson
Ultramarine
Yellow Ochre
Burnt Sienna
Vandyke Brown
White
Payne's Grey

White over
Burnt Sienna

Yellow Ochre
over White

Ultramarine and White mix
over White, Alizarin Crimson
and Payne's Grey mix

The turbulent sky is as much the subject of the painting as the architecture in this challenging composition of the Thames. The overlaid glazes of white in the sky are echoed in the overlaid brushstrokes of white on the bridge and rooftops, which bring the whole painting together without the need for too much accuracy. The river is a thin glaze of Burnt Sienna overlaid with another thin glaze of Violet, giving movement to the dark waters.

6 NEUTRALS

Vibrant, intense colours in a painting are exciting, but they are not suitable for every subject – sometimes you will want the subtle, quiet effects that come from using neutral colours.

Mixing neutrals

Your set of paints will probably contain some brown pigments, known as earth colours, because they are indeed derived from types of earth. These act as neutral colours that are ideal for providing the subtle tones in the landscape and in buildings made from stone or brick. You will also want to use them for modifying brighter colours.

However, you will gain a much wider variety of neutral browns and greys by mixing your own from opposite colours on the wheel (see page 41). In the mixes shown here you can see the difference between the warm and cool neutrals. The warm and cool range within each of those colours further expands your choice.

cool blue + cool orange

warm blue + warm orange

cool violet + cool yellow

warm violet + warm yellow

cool red + cool green

warm red + warm green

BEARDED MAN

Skin tones are subtle and need a range of neutral mixes, not just the browns available in your paint set. The deep shadows in this painting are from the range of mixes shown opposite.

Brown mixes

We are all attracted to bright, intense colour, but quieter colours are needed too for a change of mood or for subject matter such as an old stone wall, an autumn scene or a sombre day.

In your basic tube colours you will already have neutrals such as Burnt Sienna, Vandyke Brown and Yellow Ochre, known as earth colours because they come from natural clays. In addition to these you can gain a lot more control in your paintings by mixing your own very subtle browns, using the principle that opposite or complementary colours on the wheel neutralize each other.

With browns, always remember that you are aiming for warmth, so use the warmer reds, yellows, greens and blues to get the brown that you want, handling the ratio with care and attention. Mixing the main colours in the whole painting to make your brown neutrals will also make the whole painting come together.

COLD DAY, WARM HILLS

The sky, although grey, had touches of warmer neutrals within it nearer the horizon. Here, I added White to the mixes of warm violet and warm yellow. The foreground stretch of field was a mix of warm blue and warm orange, with the latter playing the bigger part.

Grey mixes

Mixing your own greys will provide you with an array of subtle colours that will suit the tones of your painting and bring your subject to life.

To mix your own greys, combine any of the primaries with its complementary – for example, combine red with green, blue with orange or purple with yellow. The two pigments cancel each other out to produce a grey. Cool greys are typically of a green or blue hue while warm greys can be mixed from red or yellow paints. You will soon gain enough control to be able to mix exactly the colour you want.

By adding white to these mixes you can alter the tint from dark to light (see page 147).

Setting off the greys with a bright, vibrant colour enhances a painting even further, as the colours are working together rather than competing. For example, a grey that has been mixed by combining green and red, as in the painting shown opposite, will be further enhanced by the addition of red (as shown in the distance) or green (as shown in the grassy foreground field).

GREY NORFOLK

The grey of the sky contains elements of both the red in the horizon and the green in the grassy foreground, creating a cohesive but vibrant scene.

Black and white mixes

The tonal value of any colour can be varied by adding White to lighten it or Black to make it darker. However, adding Black drains the original hue and sometimes produces a completely different colour, for example Lemon Yellow and Black creates an interesting green while Cadmium Red mixed with Black appears as rich dark brown – neither mix is just a dark version of the original colour.

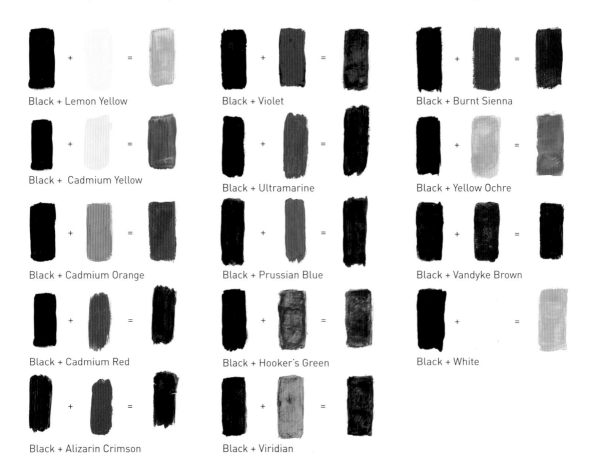

Black + Lemon Yellow

Black + Cadmium Yellow

Black + Cadmium Orange

Black + Cadmium Red

Black + Alizarin Crimson

Black + Violet

Black + Ultramarine

Black + Prussian Blue

Black + Hooker's Green

Black + Viridian

Black + Burnt Sienna

Black + Yellow Ochre

Black + Vandyke Brown

Black + White

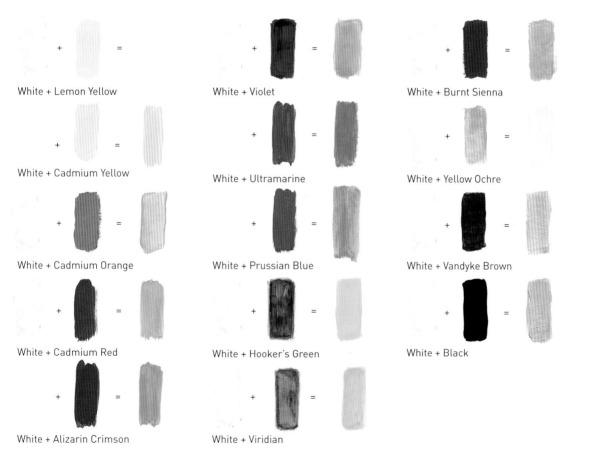

White + Lemon Yellow

White + Cadmium Yellow

White + Cadmium Orange

White + Cadmium Red

White + Alizarin Crimson

White + Violet

White + Ultramarine

White + Prussian Blue

White + Hooker's Green

White + Viridian

White + Burnt Sienna

White + Yellow Ochre

White + Vandyke Brown

White + Black

FRENCH WINDOW

White mixes have been used in the areas around the window and the objects on the table to bring a sense of light and space to the painting.

FROM THE SOUTH
BANK, LONDON

This is primarily a tonal painting.
Buildings offer a good opportunity to
clearly demonstrate light and shade.

7 COLOUR, LIGHT AND SHADE

Although, in time, you will develop your own personal palette, the colours you will use for any given painting will depend upon your subject, the location, the time of day and the mood that you wish to express. For instance, a tropical scene will call for bright colours and strong shadows, while an overcast landscape on an autumn day will require subtle hues.

Painting light

To give a painting some visual interest rather than merely representing the subject matter, showing the effect of light on your subject is vital. Outdoors the light obviously changes according to the time of day, while indoors you can take control of the direction and strength of light.

You will have noticed that colours and tones are modified both by their surroundings and by the prevailing light, and it's vital to see the colours in terms of the tonal weight of one colour against another to achieve interesting contrast in your paintings. Try to limit the colours you use and search for the bright, light colours against the stronger, darker ones so the contrast gives greater impact. Too many colours too near in tone just makes for confusion, so amend reality if you need to.

CHINESE POT AND STREPTOCARPUS
Here, I used two complementary colours, yellow and violet, to create colour contrast. The long grey shadows were exaggerated to take on a more blue-violet colour, giving a sense of drama.

HIGH KEY

Paintings are described as high key on account of their subject matter – for example, a summer border full of brightly coloured annual flowers – or because there is a feeling of strong light. The sharper the light, the more dramatic and pure the colours will appear. The bright, clear light of morning increases the strength of the hues, creating more dramatic contrast between darks and lights.

In the afternoon the light can bleach out the colours, making them paler. Nevertheless, you can use the same colours, just mixing them with white to produce tints that are a less vivid version of the original colour. Another way of keeping a painting high key is to prime the surface with a strong colour and paint on top, letting the undercolour to come through on occasion.

Painting the same location in different weather conditions and at different times of day is a fascinating project to undertake and it will also improve your skills of observation and accuracy of colour mixing.

CHAIR AND TABLE

High-key colours work so well with interesting darks. Here the reds, yellows and oranges sing out from the dark mix used for the interior walls and floor.

GARDEN

PALETTE USED

Lemon Yellow
Cadmium Yellow
Cadmium Orange
Cadmium Red
Alizarin Crimson
Violet
Ultramarine
Prussian Blue
Hooker's Green

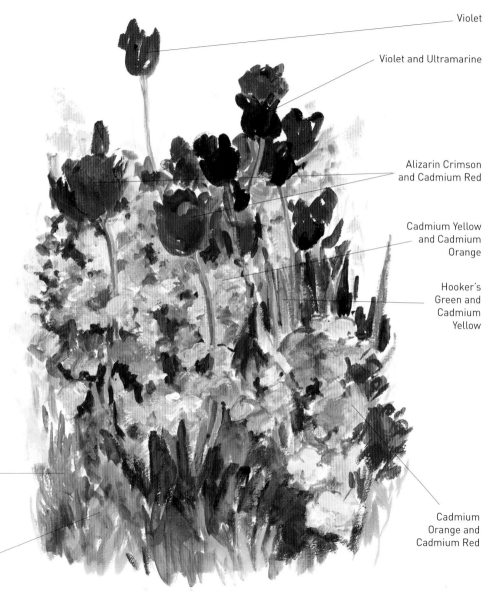

Violet

Violet and Ultramarine

Alizarin Crimson
and Cadmium Red

Cadmium Yellow
and Cadmium
Orange

Hooker's
Green and
Cadmium
Yellow

Lemon Yellow and
Prussian Blue

Prussian Blue

Cadmium
Orange and
Cadmium Red

LOW KEY

In contrast to the bright, strong colours of high-key pictures, low-key paintings rely on subtly applied unsaturated tints of colour.

English painters are known for their muted, sensitive colours that are derived more from the weather conditions than any particular artistic temperament; the melancholy mood that pervades their landscapes and seascapes reflects the influence of the climate. Contrast is reduced by the misty atmosphere and diffused light, so the tonal range is narrower than in sunny scenes, which are characterized by strong darks and lights.

You can still use pure colours if they are mixed with White and Black or applied in washes, overlaid to create a more transparent type of painting. Alternatively, you can use neutrals by carefully mixing low-key complementaries; this will give you some very luminous greys.

To give a painting an overall low-key feel, you can also reverse the procedure for a high-key painting: this time, prime the surface with a neutral colour and paint on top, letting the undercolour come through on occasion.

SOUTH DOWNS, SUSSEX
(LEFT)

The colours used are deliberately muted and employ a range of yellows, greens and browns that are very close in tone.

NORFOLK SKY
(RIGHT)

The low key is made more dramatic by the slash of warm golden orange on the stretch of land as opposed to the purple-grey in the sky. The main tonal range is similar apart from this area.

Light and shade

The term 'colour temperature' refers to how warm or cool a colour is. As you have learned, red, orange and yellow are generally regarded as warm, while blue, green and violet are cool. But within each colour range there can be warm and cool versions, and to develop your understanding of this it is worth studying the qualities of the colours used in the mixes shown in this book to gain control over your pigments and use them appropriately.

However, what really determines the warmth or coolness of any given colour in a subject is the colour of the ambient light, the reflected light from any nearby surfaces and the light source itself. Late afternoon sunlight gives subjects a warm glow and shadows are contrastingly cool; a winter's day often has a bleached, bleak sky that drains the colour from the landscape. Artificial light also has its differences; the traditional incandescent bulbs shed warm yellow light, while most low-energy bulbs are colder and standard fluorescent lighting is greenish cool.

ASLEEP
The folds and shadows of the bedcover and the dark background create warmth in the painting as well as movement and drama.

SKYSCRAPERS
AT NIGHT

Strong bright colours are
set against the cool dark
shadows to create a lively
composition that is
full of movement.

Always observe the light carefully so that you can portray a particular place and time of day successfully. You may need to make a determined effort to avoid just painting what your brain tells you; for example, you may know that a tree is green, but as it is affected by the light it may become more yellow in sunlight or more blue in shade.

THE FOREST

The figure set against the dappled light of the forest has a 'halo' of light as she is *contre-jour* or 'against the light'.

SEASHORE

The light areas in the ripples of water and the white shirt are tinted with warm reds and pinks, giving a sense of the end of day.

8 FINDING YOUR SUBJECT

As a novice artist, you may wonder where you can find interesting subjects to paint. In fact, your subject can be anything at all; the interest in a painting comes from your approach and use of colour.

If the emphasis is on strong colour, use high-key colours to give your painting impact. This could be a still life composed of brightly coloured pots and exotic plants or a beach scene with umbrellas, towels and people in typical primary colours. In garden scenes, look for the shapes and patterns in garden furniture and flowers. Light plays an important role; applying the paint in intense, smaller brushstrokes, letting the white of the primer show in between marks, creates more contrast and thus stronger 'pings' of colour.

Conversely, if you want to express a mood of tranquillity, go for a subtle painting with low-key mixes such as a mellow autumn landscape or a corner of a lamp-lit room, painted in overlaid glazes and neutrals to make a range of modified colours.

TUSCAN VALLEY
(FAR RIGHT)
The contours of the valley were too warm to convey distance, so bold colour was used in the foreground to give perspective.

TREE WITH SHADOW
(RIGHT)
To convey bright summer light the shadows needed to be deep and dark with a hint of violet to contrast with the yellow-green grass.

GARDEN GAZEBO
Here, the building draws the eye from the plants and flowers and the sense
of distance is emphasised by the blurred forms that are further away.

DISTANT HILLS
(ABOVE)
Strong brushmarks give the valley in the foreground a sense of depth, while the green contrasts with the distant fields of Alizarin Crimson, Yellow Ochre and Burnt Sienna.

POND, HAMPSTEAD
(FOLLOWING PAGE)
Water is such an interesting subject to paint, and this composition provides opportunities to contrast horizontal brushstrokes against the verticals of the trees as well as the cool water against the warm woodland.

Landscape

Even if you do not live in scenic countryside, you probably have regular access to parks or other open land that will allow you to paint the natural world. The palette you use will depend on the light and season and whether you are painting a detail or aiming for a feeling of space. Even in winter, the landscape will challenge you with a variety of greens, which can be difficult to mix successfully. While this may seem a tough task, at least at first, it means you will be using a limited palette, which gives a painting coherence.

Still life

When it comes to still life, your subject may be anything from a bowl of beautiful fruit in harmonious colours to the mundane ingredients of your dinner laid out on a chopping board. In interiors the light levels tend to be lower and the furniture may be in neutral colours, so here it will be how to express the shadows that is the challenge. Try throwing some complementary colour into these shadows for added zing. Some violet in the shadow of a yellow cup will do the trick, for example.

DAFFODILS AND PEARS

The combination of perspective (looking down on the table) and use of harmonious colours makes this a pleasing composition.

GREEN JUG AND YELLOW CUP

The old-fashioned furniture and china had such unusual shapes that they made a striking composition.

STREET SCENE, LONDON
(RIGHT)
These neutral colours are close in tone but are lifted by echoing the blue tones of the sky.

BUILDINGS, SOUBES
(LEFT)
Sky blue accents give the contrast needed to convey bright sunlight and offset the warm Yellow Ochre and White creamy walls.

Buildings

Generally speaking, buildings are in neutral colours of stone, brick, concrete and even steel and glass. Rather than relying on a manufacturer's pigments, mix unusual greys and browns of your own (see pages 140–145). Since the shadows in an urban scene are usually cast by other buildings, they are likely to be solid and hard-edged; notice that if the buildings are surrounded by trees, the shadows are more diffuse and subtle. Remember that even the darkest shadow on an urban building will have colour in it, which you can either discover by close observation or choose yourself to suit the rest of your painting and the mood you wish to create.

People

The human figure presents the most challenging subject because unless you can persuade people to pose for you, you will find they are constantly moving or changing their position, even when sitting down. Taking photographs and making sketches is helpful, and using them for reference rather than painting directly from the subject can be very liberating. You can also use your photographs as an inspiration rather than trying to make an accurate representation, which will encourage you to develop your own personal language, particularly if you exaggerate and alter the colours instead of merely copying them.

THIERRY AND BANJO
Working from a photograph was necessary for this painting as the musician subject moves so much.

UNEASY WOMAN

Painting people may seem a challenge, but choosing a limited palette of skin tones and simplifying the tones of light and shade make the process easier.

ON A CHAIR

Life classes can be very useful for quick sketches and studies in shape and tone.

ON A SOFA

Broad brushstrokes of pinks and purples and a brush outline manage to convey this figure with just a few details.

INDEX